I0408842

The Prospects Ahead

EIR Contents

www.larouchepub.com Volume 44, Number 7, February 17, 2017

Cover
This Week

Sunset *by*
Frederic Edwin
Church

MICHAEL STEGER

It's a New World

The following is an edited transcript, taken from remarks given by Michael Steger to the LaRouche PAC Manhattan Meeting of Feb. 11, 2017.

The level of changes that are taking place so quickly is almost breathtaking. We're three weeks now into a new administration, and as Mr. LaRouche had said after the election in November, this is clearly a global revolution, a global process. It wasn't something only occurring or developing in the United States.

What I'd like to go through are a couple of key developments. There is so much taking place, and I want to review some of it, put an emphasis on it, and then capture what are the restrictions.

• Why is Glass-Steagall not at the forefront of a policy discussion?

• Why is the National Bank not yet at the forefront of a policy discussion in the United States?

I think, as many of you in this room know, a big portion of this is on the level of an asymmetrical warfare on information—or really an attack on ideas and an attack on the human mind that has been taking place inside the mass media, so we'll get at that question, because it is a critical component of how we make this breakthrough and consolidate what's taking place. But before we do that, let's review the political situation.

We'll start with this recent summit that President Trump and Japanese Prime Minister Abe had, because this clearly indicated a completely new shift in the way the world is now beginning to interact—the way that major nations of this world are beginning to interact. To put a certain context to that, we recently discovered in our own *Executive Intelligence Review* magazine, an article from 1982 that situates this summit— that it was Prime Minister Abe's father who was then Minister of Trade for Japan, working with the same Mitsubishi Corporation that Lyndon LaRouche

and this organization were collaborating with on a project in Thailand to build the Kra Canal. [Abe's father] was then going to go to Florida to discuss with the G-7 nations' trade ministers, a program for a $50 billion Global Infrastructure Fund.

The projects on that list included: the Lake Chad project, which is now under discussion by China, the Kra Canal project, the Nicaragua Canal project, and the greening of the Sahara Desert. And they identified that the greatest risk to world peace was the economic deterioration and lack of development.

Now, that was Prime Minister Abe's father. It's important to make that note, simply because it is Prime Minister Abe who over the last eleven months has had a series of discussions with President Putin, and the first one last year took place in May. This is important to note, because after Abe had announced that he was planning to travel to Russia, then-President Obama had attempted to weigh in on Prime Minister Abe, and told him, "Don't go; wait for the summit you and I are going to have soon there in Japan. Wait for that first. Let me tell you what I think about this summit with Putin, and then maybe you can go." Abe said, "That's okay, I think I'll go."

At that point, you saw what was the beginning of a

kremlin.ru

Japan Prime Minister Abe (right) had met three times with President Putin (left), prior to his meeting with President Trump: May 6, 2016 in Sochi, Sept. 2, 2016 in Vladivostok, and in Nagato, Japan on Dec. 15, 2016.

major strategic shift on the planet, where nations which were closely tied to this Anglo-American program—this British imperial policy—were showing clear signs of breaking, of working now instead with this Eurasian-centered process around Russia and China. Since that summit, Abe and Putin have now met three times—first in Sochi, then again in Vladivostok, and then again in Tokyo.

At the summit in Tokyo, or soon thereafter, the Prime Minister made it clear that it was his intention that he would finally sign a peace treaty with Russia, that he would resolve the questions of the Northern Islands or Kuril Islands, as they are known in Russia—which is a territorial dispute between Russia and Japan—that he wanted to be the Prime Minister who signed that treaty, resolved Japan's sovereignty on this question, and opened up a collaboration with Russia.

So, Abe staked his own personal career on the commitment that he wanted to be the one who solved this, which clearly is in this overall orientation that we see even from his own family.

Now these things are not just governed by those local circumstances. Clearly, they're governed by a much higher process globally.

At the time, President Putin responded, and said, in effect: It's important to note that on the question of these disputed islands, the Soviet Union had already been willing to resolve this in the 1950s, but at that time, it was American influence which disrupted any type of negotiations between the Soviet Union and Japan.

They had already agreed to provide Japan with the two southern islands—there are four of them—the two southern ones would go to Japan. But John Foster Dulles, of the Wall Street-British crowd, threatened Japan, saying, if you make a deal with the Soviet Union, we will take Okinawa as U.S. property and U.S. dominion—the far southern island with the U.S. military base in Japan. So it was a direct threat, a direct intervention on the British system's behalf to prevent any kind agreement between the Soviet Union and Japan at that time.

White House

President Trump (right) made the new U.S. policy shift clear at the Feb. 10 summit in Washington, D.C. with Japan Prime Minister Shinzo Abe (left). Trump indicated that the United States would not interfere in Japan/Russia efforts to work out their differences, dating from World War II.

It is very interesting that during this summit between Trump and Abe, that this is the context that is now under discussion. President Trump made it very clear that we will not interfere, that Japan and Russia are close neighbors, they have certain interests at stake between them, and the United States will not be intervening, regarding the negotiations between Russia and Japan—you're now seeing that with the United States free of Obama, we are now permitting this kind of new system in the Eurasian world to consolidate.

At the same time, in this summit between Trump and Abe, there is a substantial discussion, in many ways, of major infrastructure development of the United States. Trump, on the day prior to the summit, was meeting with airline executives, and he said, "You go to China, you go to Japan. There are all these high-speed rails, there are all these fast trains, and in the United States, we have none." This is part of the discussion. Abe made the comment that if we built a maglev rail between Washington, D.C. and New York City, it would take one hour to get there.

This discussion of infrastructure was there—and I'll touch on that in a second—because what is critical to this is our initiative here in the United States on economic policy, for Glass-Steagall and a National Bank.

But in the broader scope of the process—because it is global—a question comes from a Japanese reporter, asking President Trump about the tensions between Japan and China, and China's growing role in the region. Of course, there's the South China Sea, and there's also these rocks out there in the East China Sea, which are disputed between China and Japan.

Trump's response was very important. He said, "I had a discussion with President Xi last night. It was a very warm discussion, very cordial, and I think that U.S.-China collaboration will be very important for the United States and China, but also for the entire region including Japan." So he made it very clear that there is this quality of discussions between Japan and Russia, between Japan and the United States, and now between the United States and China.

This was the first discussion between President Trump and President Xi since the November election, and it was clearly something of a commitment by President Trump toward the One China policy, that Taiwan and China are one nation—but it also occurred in the broader context of this new developing system. This is very important because *we are talking about the development of a system, and of a world, that has never existed before*. There is no parallel.

We can draw comparisons, we can make notes of other moments in human history where similar substantial transformations have occurred, something like the Italian Renaissance—but what is developing has never existed on the planet. So, the fellow Americans that we are organizing, the members of Congress, whoever they might be, in any institutions, throughout Manhattan, throughout New York City—there's no nostalgia.

You know, there is a big nostalgia culture we have today. But there's not even nostalgia for a great relationship between the United States and Russia, even though we had one. You have an outreach between President Trump and Xi Jinping, representing the two largest economies in the world, which is now taking new footing. Then, in addition to this, we know there has been ongoing discussion on the question of Russia, and I think we have to highlight the kind of stance that Trump has taken. The interview that Trump did with Fox News on Super Bowl Sunday,— this is the first time since the 9/11 attacks, that a President has outright condemned the Iraq War in these terms, as a "policy of murder"— that this was an injustice, that this was a criminal act.

This was an important break, and it was provoked because of the hysteria being directed against this new administration's ongoing relationship and discussions with Russia. Coming up next week, the new Secretary of State, Rex Tillerson, will probably be meeting with Russian Foreign Minister Lavrov, and they will be dis-

cussing a possible summit between Trump and Putin. They will be discussing the questions of Ukraine, of Syria, and opportunities for major collaboration between the United States and Russia.

Over the course of this last week, there were also major discussions between the United States and Turkey. Turkey is now in discussions with Russia and Iran on the question of Syria, so if the United States begins to work with Turkey more closely, it brings the United States into discussions with Russia on Syria, and also Iran.

Okay, so that's quite a situation.

As many people know, there will be a summit in May in Beijing, a Belt-and-Road summit. Helga Zepp-LaRouche just gave an interview to the Chinese government news agency *Xinhua,* and this is in the context of that summit in May. Vladimir Putin will be attending. Chinese President Xi Jinping will be hosting it. And there are now reports coming from a leading Chinese expert on the New Silk Road, in discussion with an Indian newspaper, that President Trump will be attending—although that has not yet been confirmed by either the Chinese Foreign Ministry or the U.S. State Department.

But clearly this is the kind of potential we're consolidating, and when you bring together this level of nations and heads of nations, in the context of what's now developing, we clearly have a potential over the coming weeks and months, going into the summit in May, to consolidate what Helga Zepp-LaRouche had said to the audience just last Saturday, here in Manhattan: that we are now looking at a potential for a major transformation of the world, and if President Trump has the courage to follow through on this potential—something that Mr. and Mrs. LaRouche have created over this last forty years—that if President Trump follows through on this potential today, he will clearly become a towering giant in the process of human history.

A Long-Awaited War on Drugs

The media have blacked all of this out entirely. But there's also another factor, and that is the culture itself in the United States. And the very foundation of this culture that we see today, this rotting culture—you see it in Wall Street, you see it in Washington, D.C., you see it throughout the country, the destruction and devastation of the country. It's epitomized by the drug culture, by this drug addiction. This is something for which again, Mr. LaRouche and this organization initiated specifically the war on the drugs; *we called for it*. And at the center of our call for a war on drugs, was our recognition that what was really controlling this international drug trade was the international banking institutions.

Now this is being taken up. With President Trump's recent announcements, there is now a real war on drugs, a full commitment. Well, I wouldn't say a full commitment. A full commitment has to be centered against the banks, against the role of Wall Street. We've already documented the role of HSBC, the role of Wachovia—now Wells Fargo—and these other various banks directly, in laundering drug money, and terrorist money-laundering, so that's the question. But you're now seeing a commitment.

I want to read something from President Trump which he said in a meeting with police chiefs and sheriffs earlier this week. He said:

It's time to dismantle the gangs terrorizing our citizens, and it's time to ensure that every young American can be raised in an environment of decency, dignity, love and support. You have asked for the resources, tools and support you need to get the job done. We will do whatever we can to help meet those demands. That includes a zero tolerance policy for acts of violence against law enforcement. As part of our commitment to save communities, we will also work to address the mental health crisis. Prison should not be a substitute for treatment.

We will fight to increase access to life-saving treatment to battle the addiction to drugs, which is afflicting our nation like never, ever before. I've been here two weeks; I've met a lot of law enforcement officials. Yesterday, I brought them into the Oval Office. I asked a group, what impact do drugs have in terms of a percentage on crime? They said, '75-80%.' That's pretty sad. We're going to stop the drugs from pouring in. We're going to stop those drugs from poisoning our youth, from poisoning our people. We're going to be ruthless in that fight. We have no choice. And we're going to take that fight to the drug cartels, and we will work to liberate our communities from the terrible grip of violence.

That's definitely a commitment on this drug war that we haven't seen in a very long time. And I think, prob-

White House/Pete Souza

Slavery of the U.S. populations' minds by more than 15 years of perpetual wars, and a policy of drone attacks and murders: ex-Presidents Barack Obama (left) and George W. Bush.

ably, many people in this room are aware, that as much as Ronald Reagan and his close collaborators were committed to a similar fight—then Vice-President George H.W. Bush and the Bush gang were the ones running crack cocaine into the inner cities of our country. They were running the Iran-Contra cocaine operations into the United States. So you had sabotage at that time, even in Reagan's administration, against waging a war on drugs—promoting drugs.

And so this is a fundamental shift, that we have not seen since the drug culture began in the 1960s. And now, at the same time, you have a commitment by Secretary of Homeland Security, John Kelly. He made clear statements in his testimony to Congress that we've got to execute this, we've got to shut down the drug demand. You can't eliminate it, but you've got to reduce it. We've done it before; we know how to do it.

And what we know, is that this means a development program. You have to keep these young men out of prisons, to keep them off drugs. You have to change the educational program. You have to create a sense of science and optimism throughout our education and our culture.

You have to have a program of development, of jobs—real jobs, not these makeshift jobs, not this "gig economy" as they now call it. But a sense of what you're contributing in your daily work efforts, as something significant and positive for the society as a whole. That's how we eradicate this drug culture. But you also have to go after the production of it: Ninety-nine percent of the heroin comes through the Mexican border, he said. These things have to be shut down.

Now, at the same time that this administration is committed to shutting down the drug trade, they are also willing to address the fact that the entire environmentalist program is a fraud and a scheme. Ben Deniston just did a video report on the LaRouche PAC website, which highlights what they're calling "Climategate II."

Prior to the recent, big climate-hoax summit in Paris, which received international support, a leading figure of the U.S. National Oceanic and Atmospheric Agency (NOAA) came out and leaked the proof that the Paris report on ocean water temperatures was an entirely fraudulent document. This administration is going directly after this environmentalist insanity—that it is a program for depopulation, it is a program of drug addiction, and it is a program of no-development of any sort.

And these developments are substantial, because this is the first time we've had an attack directly on the drug culture of the United States *and* an attack on this environmentalist insanity. This is the first time that this has happened. And I can tell you, I'm speaking to you from California today: There is a freakout in California, and though they might want to say it's about illegal immigration or gay rights, or gay marriage, or rights to abortion—I guarantee you: the core of this freakout is the drugs. And you wouldn't have anybody believing in so-called global warming if they weren't on drugs—if they weren't on drugs or if there wasn't a drug culture. Much of the fraud of our culture today is largely based on the idea that you've got a drug culture: It's the music, it's the pessimism, it's the loss of clarity of mind.

This brings us back to why this organization has been able to prevail in this fight over the course of these forty and fifty years: Because it wasn't simply that we didn't like the Vietnam War, or that we didn't like Obama. This organization has been led by a distinct quality of thinking, that Mr. LaRouche himself has embodied.

Now, the bigger question is this: If the population were not drugged up, no one would tolerate Wall Street bailouts. If people weren't on these drugs—and this is a broad portion of the population—you wouldn't tolerate these actions, you wouldn't tolerate the destruction of your country. You wouldn't watch the industry break down; you wouldn't watch the nation go into wars for fifteen-plus years—perpetual war. You wouldn't watch the bailouts to the very criminals that ran the criminal fraud against your population, and you wouldn't tolerate Obama's ongoing drone attacks and murder policy. So, what we're getting at is a real question here—that this question of liberating the minds of our population is something that Mr. LaRouche, Mrs. LaRouche, and this organization, and everyone who's been a member has been fighting for—a liberation of the human mind: The slavery today is a slavery of the mind.

Because what we're talking about is having access to the future. Very few Americans today have an emotional connection to the kind of future that we can build and create. That might be a little bit more understandable when there's not much there on the horizon in terms of a new potential. But today, what we've seen consolidated over these last few years, and especially with the Brexit and then the Presidential election, is now a new potential that is clearly more than just possible. It's approximating everything this organization has been fighting for. And there has to be an emotional connection to the reality that we can address the problems that mankind has feared to face for too long.

For example, the kind of poverty and famine and wars that people still imagine Africa to be. As we saw with the Ethiopia-Djibouti rail line, China has a vision of Africa far different from just wars and famine. But many people in Europe and the United States accept "that's just how Africa is." We've lost our vision, we've lost our sense of the future.

And this is really the target of this drug culture—it's to undermine the ability of the human mind to access the future, including among people who have become addicted to drugs, or dominated by the culture and by the music, by the scientific frauds, or among the people whose families are broken down by it, or whose employees are destroyed by it.

Glass-Steagall and Hamilton

This brings us back now to the single unifying question of what we've got to do to address this problem. The mobilization for Glass-Steagall and for Lyndon LaRouche's "Four Laws" is now the primary focus we have to implement, for two very clear reasons.

It is *the* inflection point of this entire political process. On the one hand, if you're going to shut down the criminal drug trade, the scientific fraud of global warming, and operators like George Soros, like the

Wall Street banks, and like what we've seen from Prince Charles in the push for the global warming fraud—then we're going to suffocate and shut down the funding for these types of operations, and we're going to shut down the drug-running.

There was a former UN official, Antonio Mario Costas, who made it very clear—and other people have corroborated this—that the banks are dependent on the hard cash of the international drug trade. With Glass-Steagall, we are going to wipe out the Wall Street gambling process. We're going to wipe out these worthless debts, and we're going to ensure the stability of the American population. That's Glass-Steagall. You have to wipe out the British system.

Now, at the same time, Glass-Steagall is the first step for the United States to take, to make it possible for Trump to join fully in a new relationship among nations, to establish a direct participation—economically and financially—of the United States in collaboration with Russia, China, Japan, and other major nations. Glass-Steagall is the first step.

The second step is a national banking system, and then you have the opportunities for the public credit and the science driver programs that are so key. Now this national banking is the very principle of the United States. Every time it's been called back into existence in some form, there has been a transformation of the American economy. And there's a very clear reason why. Today, we have a *monetary system,* a system where money circulates based on a British liberal conception of mankind, that at best you seek pleasure and attempt to avoid pain. That is the sum of all human decision-making and choices on a social level and on economic practices. That's how the British economic system views their so-called statistical principle within economics.

But the very opposite is true: Human beings are not governed according to that process. We have unique access to the power of the human mind to identify the longer-ranging and more substantial principles that govern our universe, our development, and our culture. We have access to recognize and identify those principles, to discover them as new, and to act upon them toward the benefit of the society and of mankind as a

FIRNS/Stefan Tolkedorf

Helga Zepp-LaRouche (left) and EIR's *Washington, D.C. correspondent Bill Jones, in Beijing, China Sept. 29, 2015, for the release of the Chinese-language translation of* EIR's *World Land-Bridge report.*

whole. The National Bank does that. It takes the so-called "money supply" that's been thrown out there by these bailouts, through these printing presses, and it shuts that process down, and it aggregates that money supply and transforms it into a credit system. It changes the system—it becomes an inflection point, or a change. So that that money is aggregated with a singular focus of development of the country as a whole. That is an aggregate power of the nation as a whole and its future, to develop that future.

This is a Credit System, not a Monetary System. That's why the National Bank becomes so important,— that we take the money that's in circulation, we take the Treasury bonds that are in circulation, and you now bring them to bear for development. As you see in New York City, I see it here in the San Francisco Bay Area. Where does a lot of the money go that directly affects us? It goes into hyperinflation of basic commodities, and into things like real estate—that's a major area.

Under a national banking Hamiltonian economy, under a LaRouche policy, that investment loses money. It's becoming obsolete. It's a slumlord-like approach to economics, to put your money into so-called real estate as some kind of long-term financial investment. A true economy is one based on the conception of the principle of mankind, which governs this new system—this new relationship among nations. The true economy is one where you're having a transformation of technology, creating advanced technologies and making the previous technologies obsolete. That's where you find your greatest profit! That's where you find your greatest return on investment! In the areas like fusion technology, space exploration, as in what Kesha raised on the 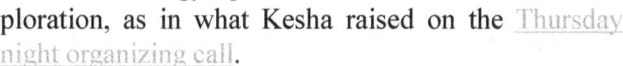Thursday night organizing call.

The New System of the Future

These questions of major scientific and technological advancement, of high-speed rail, of a development of land area, something like the Bering Strait Tunnel, to develop the areas of the Far East, Siberia, and the northwest parts of Alaska and Canada and the United States,—these sorts of technologies and projects create a new economy and a new society. So instead of having money oriented towards the places where people can make some kind of quick gain, on very obsolete and static entities—or even worse, as we know, the drug trade—instead, the national banking system transforms that and reorients it towards a real advancement of the development of the country. And that's a sense of principle. That's a sense of what the human mind can grasp—that capability. And that's why it's always been such a powerful aspect of the United States economy.

It's this drug culture that we've now seen for over fifty years in this country—promoted and endorsed as somehow "expanding your mind"—that we are now going to end, this British system, and orient to what is very clearly, on an international level, a major development orientation with major nations—and this includes nations like Mexico. Homeland Security Secretary John Kelly made it clear that we've got to work with Mexico. China has offered to work with Mexico in questions of high-speed rail and port development.

Representative Marcy Kaptur website

Reps. Marcy Kaptur (D-Ohio, speaking), Walter Jones (R-N.C.), Tim Ryan (D-Ohio, left) and Tulsi Gabbard (D-Hawaii, right) call for re-instatement of the Glass-Steagall Act, Feb. 1, 2017.

These are the parallels between the projects under discussion today, and what this organization has promoted and developed over fifty years, from *Operation Juárez* to the collaboration on the *International Development Bank*. These projects are now coming to fruition, but not as separate projects, but as a unified, integral system of human development. And it's that kind of political fight, around Glass-Steagall, that then becomes the inflection point to eliminate and destroy this British system, and to create the kind of new system which can clearly be consolidated over the coming weeks, and potentially at the Belt and Road Initiative summit in May, with the level of representation that might be developing there.

It's striking. And the way that we saw that Glass-Steagall developed last week—at the press conference led by Rep. Marcy Kaptur—you saw a bipartisan effort; you saw a commitment to work with the new Presidency, to break this so-called partisan political theater you currently see—the political theater of George Soros at the airports and these protests. Instead, you saw people cutting through that, to focus on the needed policy, and to state that they were going to work together, in bipartisan fashion, with this new administration to bring this policy to bear.

And then, over this last week, you see the consolidation of these international developments:
- the war on drugs,
- collaboration with Japan,
- collaboration with Russia,
- collaboration with China.

We've got a lot to do.

The 1812 Russian-American Alliance: Lessons for the Trump Administration

by Judy Hodgkiss

Feb. 13—The overturning of the policy axioms of the 2009-2017 Obama Administration—a happy result of the recent U.S. Presidential election—has now, once again, created a potential for a dramatic shift in U.S.-Russian relations, and such a breakthrough could effect a profound change for the better in world affairs. The opportunity for a needed paradigm shift is now a very real prospect before us.

The Cold-War ideology of 1945-1989, followed by Obama's demonization of Russia in the recent period, has led many Americans to believe that Russia and America are historical adversaries; but nothing could be further from the truth.

Within recent memory we have the World War II strategic/military alliance between Franklin Roosevelt and Joseph Stalin— an alliance which not only ensured the defeat of Nazi Germany, but also posed a critical challenge to the British, French, and Dutch colonial world order.

We can say that the very existence of our Union owes a debt to an earlier U.S.-Russian military alliance: during the U.S. Civil War, the Russian navy of Czar Alexander II harbored in New York and San Francisco, delivering a blunt warning to the French and British allies of the Confederacy that deterred any thoughts of interventionism.

These military/strategic combinations were not based on mere short-term convenience. The U.S.-Russia friendship has deep roots, based in events that occurred long before either the U.S. or Russia represented any kind of world-class military power.

That historical friendship is of great significance for current events. Today, Russia is assuming a leading role, together with China, Japan, India, and many other nations, in bringing into existence a global "win-win" policy of peace and economic development. Were President Trump to use this opportunity, in the context of repairing and improving U.S.-Russia relations, to fully embrace that global effort—to join, not only with Russia, but with all of her partners—the world would change for the better in ways that most individuals can not imagine.

The opportunity is before us; but the danger would be to continue into the new paradigm with the "practical thinking" suited to the old paradigm. Therefore, let us look back to the year 1812, when two great statesmen, U.S. Ambassador to Russia John Quincy Adams, and Russia's Foreign Minister Nikolai Rumiantsev, designed an alliance that was anything but practical. Our new paradigm of today will, in fact, require that those kinds of very impractical, yet very necessary ideas be brought into consideration now.

Students of history think they know what happened in the War of 1812, when the United States under President James Madison defeated an invading British army. And they think they know what happened—in an en-

Public domain
Count Nikolai Rumiantsev

Public domain
John Quincy Adams

tirely separate universe!—when, in 1812, the Russian Czar Alexander I defeated the invading armies under the command of France's Napoleon Bonaparte.

But, in 1812, while the Americans were at war with the British, and the Russians were at war with the French, it was also the case that the French and the British were at war with one another. Therefore, even the better informed historical analyst generally assumes there is no reason to even look for evidence of a Russian-American alliance: what nation would be so foolish as to ally with the friend of their mortal enemy, particularly during wartime?

But that is in fact exactly what Russia and the United States did.

During the previous three years, 1809-1811, U.S. Ambassador Adams and Foreign Minister Rumiantsev had developed a close relationship based upon a shared vision of world peace, and of joint economic prosperity. The two of them agreed that the war between France and Britain was, in fact, a war of pretense, merely a cover beneath which the two belligerents attacked and plundered the other nations of the world.

The ultimate goal of the sham "war" was a world divided: a maritime empire for Britain and a continental empire for Napoleon.[1] In his conversations with Adams, Rumiantsev described the British and the French as the sea madmen and the land madmen *(des enrages de mer comme de terre)*.

Between 1809 and 1811, in order to avoid the jealous eye of the powerful "British Party" inside the Russian court, Rumiantsev arranged for Adams to have more than a dozen "coincidental" meetings with Alexander I, as the czar took an occasional stroll through the gardens and streets of St. Petersburg. For his part, Adams then communicated the agreed upon policy to Secretary of State James Monroe, who in turn was tasked with convincing President Madison of the importance of the economic and strategic alliance with Russia.

It was, in fact, precisely because the United States and Russia were successful in helping each other, economically and strategically, during the extremities of 1811-1812, that the two nations escaped the otherwise

A. Savin

St. Petersburg residence of Count Rumiantsev. Built by his father, the bas relief portico with Apollo and nine muses of arts and sciences was installed by the count. The residence and its collections were bequeathed as a gift to the Russian people upon the count's death.

certain doom of perpetual warfare and economic devastation planned by the sea mad-men and land mad-men.

Likewise, the London/Wall Street imperial mad-men of today can be destroyed by just such a principled Russian-American strategy.

A Story Waiting To Be Told

John Quincy Adams left the evidence for all this in his many letters, dispatches, and diary entries—all of which material was painstakingly gathered together and published in many volumes by his son, Charles Francis. Why then are we today left in such ignorance on the subject? There are two answers to this question.

The major problem is that the first historical study of this period, proclaimed today generally to be the definitive interpretation of Adams' material, was written by one of the most slavish admirers of the British Empire ever born in America—John Quincy Adams' own grandson, Henry Adams, the third son of Charles Francis.

Henry Adams' mission, in his *History of the United States During the Administrations of Thomas Jefferson and James Madison* was to represent his grandfather as a weak man, who was pushed around in Russia by the

---

1. But Napoleon, of course, just like Adolf Hitler later, was never to be an equal partner of the British Empire, but merely a useful tool, disposable in the end.

© Alex Florstein Fedorov, Wikimedia Commons

The magnificent Kunstkamera of St. Petersburg, on the Neva waterfront, was built by Peter the Great to house Leibniz's Academy of Science.

evil calculator and French agent, Count Rumiantsev. In order to obscure both the nature of the British Empire's methods and the nature of the brilliant strategy developed by John Quincy Adams and Rumiantsev to fight it, Henry Adams had to lie outrageously.

The second problem is that even the small handful of historians who pay no attention to the lies of Henry Adams, and who have, in good faith, closely studied the subject, still are unable to grasp the significance of the intense strategic dialogue between Adams and Rumiantsev. One of the best of these historians, Nikolai Bolkhovitinov, wrote *The Beginnings of Russian-American Relations 1775-1815*, in the 1960s, under difficult circumstances at the height of the Cold War. Bolkhovitinov presents a sympathetic view of the 1812 Russian-American alliance in a (commendable) effort to counter what he calls, "an attempt in the West to utilize the history of Russian-American relations to foster the idea that, something like a 'natural' and 'age-long' hostility between Russia and the U.S. existed." Bolkhovitinov is particularly concerned about the rhetoric of John Foster Dulles and the influence of Cold-War books such as *America Faces Russia: Russian-American Relations from Early Times to Our Day*, by Stanford's Thomas A. Bailey, 1950, and the 1953 *Russian Influence on Early America*, by Columbia University's Clarence Manning. But Bolkhovitinov is always on the defensive and fails to grasp the true quality of the encounters between Adams and Rumiantsev.

Two other books that are worth reading are: *America, Russia, Hemp, and Napoleon: American Trade with Russia and the Baltic, 1783-1812*, Alfred Crosby, Jr. (1965), and *Distant Friends: The United States and Russia, 1763-1867*, Norman E. Saul (1991). Saul gives little space to the Adams-Rumiantsev relationship, but is a great source for the later, 1860-65 Civil War, Russian-American military alliance.

The Coincidence of Opposites

Honest histories of the subject report that the American and the Russian, from their first contact, felt an immediate affinity for one another. It may seem a strange idea that an autocratic imperial society, where a small number of landowners, an inherited nobility, reigned over a population made up largely of serfs, would warmly welcome the coming into existence of an upstart republic bent on eliminating all relics of feudal political and economic systems. It came as a surprise to the Americans visiting Russia that there existed a boundless curiosity about the American experiment, and a genuine excitement about encountering beings who were so eager to sail a mighty ocean, risk attacks from belligerents, pay large sums extorted from them by those controlling certain sea channels (i.e., the Danes), all in order to find a trading partner located at the northernmost reaches of the globe.

In 1803, before the establishment of diplomatic relations between the U.S. and Russia, Joseph Allen Smith from South Carolina entered Russia as a tourist and found that with just the mere mention that he had, in London, made the acquaintance of Rufus King, then the U.S. ambassador to Britain, and the Russian ambassador, Count Vorontsov, he was then swept up to the highest levels of the Court, including meeting Czar Alexander himself. Rufus King, a protégé of Alexander Hamilton, had been engaged in a dialogue with Vorontsov about a potential commercial treaty between Russia and the United States. Smith wrote to King after his trip,

"The marks of friendship and attention which I received in that city [St. Petersburg] were far beyond what I expected or deserved. I should say no more on this subject if I did not think that they were in many instances directed rather to the country to which I belong than to myself. At the fetes of the Court I was put on a footing with the Foreign Ministers, and often, as an American traveler, I found myself more favoured than if I had had a diplomatic character... The Emperor invited me to dine with him *en famille,* placed me next to him, and conversed with me some time respecting America and France."

John Quincy Adams arrived as America's official ambassador to Russia in 1809. Adams had been in St. Petersburg before, when he served as personal secretary to Francis Dana, appointed by the Continental Congress to the court of Catherine the Great as Minister Plenipotentiary during the American Revolution. Dana and the fifteen year-old Adams had been part of the Revolution's diplomatic representation in Paris, but as soon as Catherine announced that she would use her navy to protect neutral (American) shipping on the high seas, and was forming a League of Armed Neutrality, the Continental Congress ordered Dana and Adams to depart for St. Petersburg.

Dana was recalled as soon as the treaty was signed by Britain ending the Revolutionary War, and more than twenty years would pass before the U.S. and Russia would establish formal relations. Dana reported that he had been assured by Russian Vice Chancellor Ivan Osterman, just before his departure, that full recognition of the United States was imminent. Unfortunately, there were those in the United States who knew nothing of Russia, and questioned Catherine's motives. They asked: beyond just using the colony's rebellion as leverage against Britain for geopolitical purposes, what interest could Catherine have in a new nation founded on principles diametrically opposed to her political and economic system?

But there were others who began to study Russia's history, and found that there were a number of intriguing contradictions. Yes, Russia did maintain its feudal system long after other nations of Europe had moved beyond such backward practices; but Russian czars, starting with Peter the Great, struggled to modernize, against both the enormous power and opposition of the landed aristocracy that ruled over vast stretches of territory, and also the entrenched, anti-technology backwardness of the peasant. These czars pushed forward a variety of enlightened policies regarding the advancement of scientific knowledge and the acquisition of new technologies, and many among the nobility in St. Petersburg and Moscow were supportive. Within the Russian intelligentsia, there were those who argued that

their problem of serfdom was comparable to America's problem of slavery.[2]

In the early 1700s, Peter the Great had made efforts to reform education, liberalize the legal system, and introduce technology into agriculture. His most noted achievement was the construction of the splendid city of St. Petersburg,[3] with the Kunstkamera, the building housing the newly established Russian Academy of Sciences, at its heart. The Kunstkamera came complete with the world's most advanced astronomical observatory on its roof.

Czar Peter was advised by Gottfried Leibniz, the founder of the Berlin Academy of Sciences and the original source and inspiration for the ideas of the Founding Fathers of the United States. Leibniz had proposed the establishment of the Russian Academy of Sciences in 1711. Some of the world's most advanced studies in the areas of astronomy, meteorology, geodesy, topography, and chronography would be carried out there, with Daniel Bernoulli, Leonhard Euler, and Jakob Hermann taking up residence in St. Petersburg in order to participate.

Catherine the Great had mobilized the Academy's scientists to participate in the international measurements of the once-in-a-century phenomenon of the transit of Venus across the sun, which would provide clues to the size of the solar system. Russia set up observations in eight locations, at one of which the Academy's director, Mikhail Lomonosov, found the first evidence of an atmosphere on Venus. As part of her enthusiasm for the project, Catherine acquired for the Academy eighteen volumes of the original manuscripts of Johannes Kepler, the man who had predicted the transit one hundred years earlier.

Quincy Adams' collaborator in St. Petersburg, Count Rumiantsev, was the son of Field Marshal Peter Alexandrovich Rumiantsev, widely understood to be the illegitimate son of his godfather, Peter the Great. The field marshal and his sister were confidantes of Catherine, the sister handling Catherine's private communications.

Before becoming the foreign minister/chancellor for Alexander, Count Rumiantsev had been commerce minister (1802-1808), and had personally financed sev-

---

2. Lincoln's Emancipation Proclamation and Czar Alexander II's decree for the emancipation of the serfs occurred nearly simultaneously.
3. Adams, who had seen Paris, London, and Berlin, proclaimed St. Petersburg to be the "most magnificent city of Europe, or of the world."

eral voyages of discovery to the Pacific coast of America and to the South Pacific. Species of American butterflies and orchids were named after him, and, when the Russians claimed northern California, Bodega Bay had been Rumiantsev Bay. He also was the primary sponsor of Russia's first circumnavigation of the globe.

Upon his death, the Rumiantsev Museum was established, housing his collection of maps spanning the globe and his rare Russian historical manuscripts and books. When the capital was moved to Moscow in 1918, the Rumiantsev Mansion on the Neva waterfront was maintained as a museum with his personal effects, but his collection became the basis for the Moscow Rumiantsev Library—renamed the State Russian Library.

When Alexander I came to power in 1801, he started a new journal, called, *A Collection of Works and News Related to Technology and Applications of Discoveries Made in Science*, and he drew up new statutes and dramatically increased the funding for the Academy. Alexander stated the purpose for his actions:

"To extend the range of human knowledge, perfect the sciences, enrich them with new discoveries, promote education, direct knowledge to the common benefit... to the use of Russia directly, promoting knowledge of natural resources of Russia, discovering means of multiplying such that make up the subject of popular industry and trade, of improving the state of factories, manufactures, trades and arts—these sources of the wealth and power of states."

Before the War of 1812, Alexander arranged a contract for Robert Fulton to bring over his engineers and mechanics to build steamships for Russia. Fulton was granted a fifteen-year patent, with the proviso that the first steamship was to be built within three years; but because of the war the contract became defunct, and it was many years before Russia gained steamship technology.

During the five years that Ambassador Adams was in St. Petersburg, he often visited the Kunstkamera and exchanged communications between it and the Philosophical Society of Philadelphia, the Boston Academy of Arts and Sciences, and Harvard University. It was here that Adams developed his lifelong passion for astronomy, a passion that propelled him to a thirty-year-long fight for the establishment of a national astronomical observatory for the United States.

America Ensures Russia's Survival

When Adams came to St. Petersburg in 1809, all of Europe was at a strategic tipping point. The British Empire, in partnership with its subcontractor Napoleon Bonaparte, was ready to deliver the final blow. Napoleon had established, in 1807, the Continental System, under which each of the countries of Europe was supposed to manage its trade at Napoleon's whim. The target of Napoleon's blockade of the entire continent was ostensibly Great Britain, but, in reality, Great Britain was the main beneficiary of the system, and was consolidating control with the long-term goal of destroying the two countries at opposite ends of the earth who were still left to resist subjugation: Russia and the United States. The British plan for Russia was, under the threat of all-out war from France, the gutting of the Russian economy; the plan for the United States was perpetual low-intensity warfare with Britain, the curtailment of American trade, and, eventually, the destruction of the U.S. economy.

Who would have dreamed that America and Russia would combine to save each other?

Adams described the situation in 1810 in a letter to his brother, Thomas Boylston Adams,

> Unhappily for mankind the present state of the world exhibits the singular phenomenon of two great powers oppressing the whole species under the color of a war against each other. France and England can do very little harm comparatively speaking to each other. But the armed legions of France lay the continent of Europe under the most enormous contributions to support and enrich them, while the naval force of England extorts the same tribute from the commerce of the world...
>
> The two parties have already come to an arrangement de facto, which suits the purpose of both. All neutrality and neutral trade are by common consent of the belligerents annihilated. The British at settled prices grant licenses to any flag, French as well as any other, which are respected by her navy. The Emperor Napoleon gives licenses to any flag, English as well as any other, which are respected by all his subordinate authorities. All other commerce is proscribed, and under these double licenses the commerce between the British islands and the continent of Europe is now carried on, to an extent beyond that of the most active and prosperous times of peace. France and England both raise a large revenue from the licenses, which ultimates as a tax upon the consumption of the articles circulating by this new method of trade."

The Russians had refused to buy the required licenses needed to maintain their trade with Britain, which had been, by far, Russia's largest trading partner. The ensuing collapse of Russian trade led directly to a catastrophic drop in the value of the ruble by fifty percent between 1807 and 1810.

The policy of Rumiantsev had been to encourage the substitution of British shipping with American. The bulk of British trade with Russia had, anyway, been composed of the re-export and re-import of goods to and from America. The British picked up ship-building materials from Russia: hemp for cordage and cables; coarse linen for sailcloth and sacks; and iron for anchors, chains, barrel staves, and cannon.[4] Those items would be carried across the Atlantic, where they were exchanged for goods from the Caribbean and Brazil: sugar and coffee, mainly. Americans would trade these commodities in exchange for the Russian goods delivered by the British.

Very slowly, the Americans had developed their merchant marine to the point where they were beginning to replace the British intermediary with their own direct shipping. The table below grids the number of ships entering St. Petersburg's harbor, Kronstadt, between 1785 and 1812. In 1807 Russia signed the Tilsit Treaty with Napoleon that banned Russian-British trade.

Ships Entering Kronstadt Harbor

		British	American
	1785	640	6
	1792	517	22
	1807	—	90
	1811	—	225
(After U.S. declaration of war)	1812	36	7

In 1808, Napoleon decreed that all American-flag ships were to be considered British, and therefore to be banned. Russia ignored the decree. In 1810, Napoleon banned specifically all sugar and coffee coming into Europe and Russia, even setting bonfires to stores of those items. Russia refused to cooperate.

---

4. A forty-four gun frigate of the Constitution class needed two suits of sails, each ¾ of an acre in extent; 100 tons of hemp rope; 75 tons of iron, not counting cannon or ammunition. The Secretary of the Navy was asked in 1824, why not American hemp?, and answered: "cables and cordage manufactured from it are inferior in color, strength and durability to those manufactured from imported hemp, and consequently are not as safe or proper for use in the navy."

Adams wrote from St. Petersburg to Secretary of State Robert Smith, on Dec. 5, 1810,

The refusal of Russia to seize and confiscate, or to shut her ports against future importations of colonial articles [sugar and coffee] was communicated to the French Ambassador on the first of this month, and he immediately dispatched it by a courier to his government. The determination of the Emperor, of Count Romanzoff,[5] and of the whole Imperial Council is said to be fixed and unalterable, and I hope will prove so at the test to which I think it will be brought; but if a message comes, like that to Sweden, which is not impossible, the necessity of commerce and the real regard for the United States, which is undissembled and unimpaired, may yield to the first principle of the Russian policy at this time, which is at all events to keep on good terms with France.

Ten days later, Adams wrote,

Until lately… France has abstained from demanding of Russia measures ruinous to her own interests and derogatory to her independence. Such demands are now made, and as I have informed you have met with denial. It is not probable that France will be satisfied with this, and I think the relations between the two countries are approaching to a crisis on a point highly interesting to us.

Russia would not budge. And Russia not only survived the attempt at strangulation, she boomeranged the entire strategy back against Napoleon: Since no one in Europe could obtain a gram of coffee or sugar from any other source, Russian merchants began to smuggle the stuff overland, first into Vienna, then through all the border states, until Russian sugar found its way even into Paris. The ruble regained its losses, and more.

Upon receiving notice from the czar that he was refusing to interdict the forbidden products, Napoleon reportedly said, "Here is a great planet taking a wrong direction. I do not understand its course at all." He then wrote, in a personal letter to Czar Alexander,

For myself, I am always the same; but I am struck

---

5. Romanzoff, Roumanzoff, Rumyantsev, it is all the same person.

by the evidences of these facts, and by the thought that Your Majesty is wholly disposed, as soon as circumstances permit it, to make arrangement with England [America], which is the same thing as to kindle a war between two Empires."

In December 1811, Adams wrote to his brother,

This commercial phenomenon of colonial merchandises exported from St. Petersburg and Archangel into Germany, Italy, and even France, is one of those singular symptoms in the disordered state of the civilized world (if it deserves to be called so) which strike superficial observers with amazement. The Emperor Napoleon has been preaching abstinence of *sugar* and *coffee* to the people of Europe, with as much zeal as the hermit Peter once preached the recovery of the Holy Sepulchre from infidels... Notwithstanding all which sugar and coffee still make their way even into France... this channel of trade has been barely opened during the present year; but it has proved so advantageous, not only to the individual merchants, but to the revenues, the finances, and the credit of this empire, that it will probably be continued on a much more extensive scale the next summer, unless a new war should come and break it up altogether…

In this new state of European commerce our countrymen have hitherto been almost exclusively the carriers on the ocean... One effect of this incidental result of the continental system has been that the exchange here upon Hamburg, Amsterdam, and Paris, which nine months ago was from ten to fifteen percent below par, is now as much above it. The balance of trade which was so heavily against Russia, is now as much to her advantage. It is hardly possible however that France, perceiving this tax which she is paying

Public domain
Czar Alexander I

to Russia should submit to it, and if she can prevent it, she will probably not scruple at the means, though war should be among them.

Russia had survived the economic warfare, thanks to the Americans. Next, she had to survive the war, which she did—at least she survived the Franco-Russian War of 1812. As we will see, it was much more difficult for Russia to survive the other war of 1812, the U.S.-British one. The self-inflicted wound the U.S. suffered when she declared war against Great Britain in June, proved a difficult enough recovery for the U.S.; but in terms of Russia and the rest of the world, it was just the opening that the British Empire needed to reassert itself, in just a slightly different form; and, as we will see, by the time the war was over, Russia's czar would be the primary victim.

The Lost Opportunity

Napoleon's forces crossed the Niemen River into Russia on nearly the same day in June that the U.S. Congress voted for war against the British. The forces arrayed against Russia were truly formidable: the Duchy of Warsaw, Napoleonic Italy, Naples, Holland, the German Confederation of the Rhine, Napoleonic Spain and the Swiss Confederation, totaling nearly 600,000 men, three times the number of troops under the Russian command. The Austrians and Prussians formed independent commands, guarding the northern and southern flanks of Napoleon's army.

But Alexander had a plan. He had written a note to the French ambassador, Caulaincourt, and even told him of the plan two weeks before Napoleon invaded.

If Emperor Napoleon declares war, it is possible, even probable, that he will defeat us if we accept combat, but that will not bring him peace. The Spaniards have often been defeated and are neither conquered nor subjugated. However, they are not as distant as we are from

Paris, and they do not have our climate or our resources. We will not compromise. We have space and we shall keep a well-organized army in being... If the issue of arms goes against me, I shall retreat to Kamchatka rather than yield provinces and sign treaties in my capital that will merely be truces. The French are brave, but our privations and a bad climate would weary and discourage them. Our climate, our winter, will make war for us. Wonders are brought about for you only where the Emperor is present, and he cannot be everywhere when his armies are far from Paris."

The great military strategist, Napoleon, had met his match. The war unfolded along lines very close to Alexander's forecast: the Russian forces skirmished with the invading armies, drawing them further into the depths of Russia throughout July, August, and early September. The czar's orders to his commanders: Do not fully engage; never risk the total exhaustion of the army.

The only major battle before Napoleon entered Moscow on September 14 was fought on the field of Borodino, seventy miles from Moscow, along the Moskva River. Napoleon's forces had been decimated from disease, starvation and desertion. His supply lines were practically nonexistent, the troops fed by foraging. The battle at Borodino was particularly bloody: each side began about evenly, with around 200,000 troops, and each side losing 40-50,000 over the course of two days.

At the point Napoleon's forces seemed to be gaining the upper hand, the Russians, under the cover of the smoke and confusion, fell back, then ran. Moscow, which had been evacuated over the previous few days, was torched in several places just as Napoleon's troops entered the city. More fires were set over the next week, and most of the city burned. But Napoleon settled in: he assumed that Alexander knew that he had been beaten, and would soon respond to a letter demanding Russia's total surrender.

Alexander's surrender letter never arrived. What did arrive was Russia's winter.

On October 18, Napoleon gave the order for his half-frozen army to pack up and head home. The Russian forces harassed the retreating troops mercilessly, as they froze, starved, or just dropped dead from exhaustion. By the time that the Grand Armée reached the Niemen River, where it had started with 600,000 men,

there were only 20,000 left.

By December 1812, the Russians' defensive war was over. The other harried victims of Europe were now rising up, helping the Russians to hound Napoleon's forces back across Germany towards Paris. No nation was any longer interested in enforcing the Great Conqueror's edicts on trade.

The game was over, the jig was up: now "neutral shipping" was just normal shipping. Now the American Merchant Marine was free to expand its fleet and openly replace the British who had once dominated the harbor at Kronstadt. But,— America had declared war on Great Britain.

As can be seen by the table presented above, in 1812, American trade with Russia collapsed to practically nil, while Britain was starting to fill the gap. Even after the War of 1812 was finally settled in 1814, American shipping to Russia never fully recovered and was never able to compete with the British again for space at Kronstadt harbor.

Historian Alfred Crosby's characterization of these developments, although slightly skewed, is essentially correct in its broad sweep,

> Russo-American trade never became one of the main channels of world commerce, but in time of world crisis it has twice had great importance. The most recent occasion was, of course, during the terrible years of World War II. The other was during those momentous years between the rape of Copenhagen and the gutting of Moscow, when peaceful Yankee merchants provoked Napoleon and Alexander I to mortal combat, when the world trembled to find itself turning on an axis that ran from the docks of Boston, United States of America, to the waterfront of Kronstadt, Russia.

Russia Ensures America's Survival

In June 1811, one year before the declaration of war against Britain by the United States, Ambassador Adams wrote to the U.S. Secretary of State, James Monroe,

> On this occasion it may be proper to inform you, with the request that it may be received as in the closest secrecy, that I have recently had two accidental conversations with his Imperial Majesty [the Czar], in which he manifested the desire to be informed, what was the precise state of our

present relations with England. In the last of them, which was the day before yesterday, he told me that he had received very interesting dispatches from Count Pahlen [Russian ambassador to the U.S.], which had given him much pleasure. I have it from a good source that in those dispatches the Count gives it as his decided opinion that there will ultimately be no war between the United States and England, and I know from authority equally good that the Russian government earnestly wishes there may be no such war.

And in April, to his brother, Thomas:

We hear, and I most sincerely hope, that the non-importation act [cutting off trade with England]... did not eventually pass: It was a trap to catch us into a war with England; a war which England most richly deserves, but which would on our part be more than ever impolitic at this time.

Two months before the declaration of war, Rumi-antsev sent a letter, transmitted through Swedish Crown Prince Bernadotte, to the English diplomat, Edward Thornton:

Having studied the state of relations between Great Britain and America, His Majesty the Emperor came to the conviction that it is impossible for Great Britain not to do everything in her power to avoid war with the United States; and she cannot avoid this war if she does not revoke the so-called orders-in-council. Apparently the majority of Parliament considers their repeal advantageous, and the nation, it seems, also wishes it.

As a result, British Prime Minister Liverpool wrote a highly agitated letter to Foreign Secretary Castlereagh:

I fear the Emperor of Russia is half an American, and it would be very desirable to do away any prejudices which may exist in his mind.

What were the "orders-in-council," and how were they part of the "trap" to catch the U.S. in a war?

In 1806, Napoleon's "Berlin Decree" forbade allied or neutral ships to trade with Britain. Britain's response came from its Privy Council (hence, orders-in-council), with orders to forbid allied or neutral ships trading with France.

The result: between 1806 and 1812, Britain captured 917 American vessels, France captured 858. Both the French and the British often stole seamen from these American ships and "impressed" them into service onto their own vessels. The British were much the worse in this latter practice, claiming that many Americans were actually Englishmen who had deserted from the British navy.

But there was no dramatic increase in the harassment from the British in the twelve months before the U.S. declaration of war. The fact is, that there *was* an increase in harassment—but by the French and their Danish satrapy, not the British.

Adams wrote to his brother in December 1811,

Nothing will I trust have been done in [the Congress] to precipitate a rupture with France or England, and I hope nothing will produce it. Both of them are still doing, as they have done, their worst against us short of involving us with them in their quarrel. But all the evil they have done us is but the dross of which that would be the ocean.

The U.S. declared war on Britain on June 6, 1812. The howling irony here is that the states most involved in the business of shipping, and hence suffering the most losses in men and money, were the New England states and New York—those very states who most opposed the idea of the war. The states most aggressively pushing a declaration of war were the southern states and the frontier states of Kentucky and Tennessee. It was that combination of states, the slave states, that wanted to break the power of the northern states.

The "War Hawk" party was led by Henry Clay of Kentucky and John C. Calhoun of South Carolina. They allied with certain representatives of the northern states who were interested in the opportunity to attack Canada. The combination won the vote, but barely.

The War Hawks made wild promises. In the debate before Congress, Clay said,

It is said, however, that no object is attainable by war with Britain... The conquest of Canada is in your power. I trust I shall not be deemed presumptuous when I state, what I verily believe, that the militia of Kentucky are [able] alone to place Montreal and Upper Canada at your feet.

John C. Calhoun stated,

I believe that in four weeks from the time a declaration of war is heard on our frontier, the whole of Upper Canada and part of Lower Canada will be in our power.

Thomas Jefferson, not holding any office at the time, weighed in with a letter to the editor of Philadelphia's Jacobin newspaper, *Aurora*:

The acquisition of Canada this year, as far as the neighborhood of Quebec, will be a mere matter of marching.

For those who believe that the War of 1812 began when Britain "invaded the United States," let it be stated here that the first military action of the war was an invasion, by the United States, of Canada, only four weeks into the war. As we now know, ultimately no territory in Canada was captured. In fact, the war did not go well at all. The British knew they could not conquer the U.S.; but that was never their aim in drawing the U.S. into the conflict: The goal was the perpetual skirmishing in itself, which they hoped would end in the eventual bankruptcy of the northern and Great Lakes states who were doing the fighting, while the slave states were to remain intact.

And that was exactly where the United States was headed. Without the intervention of Czar Alexander on September 30, 1812, with an offer to mediate the conflict—an offer which caused the British to fall back on their heels—America were likely to have been eliminated as an economic power altogether.

In April 1813, President Madison announced:

We are at present occupied with the Mediation of Russia. That is the only power in Europe which

Public domain

Thomas Jefferson

Public domain

Henry Clay

Public Domain

John C. Calhoun

can command respect from both France and England; and at this moment it is in its Zenith.

By the spring of 1813, the U.S. government was on the verge of insolvency, caught between a collapse of tax revenue and the need for outgoing payments to build up the navy. Madison's publicizing of the Russian mediation offer worked like a charm to revive confidence, as recorded in a report written by Russian Consul-General in Philadelphia, Nikolai Kozlov, and sent to Rumiantsev:

Since then [since Madison's announcement of the Czar's intention] obstacles to the loan [to the U.S. government] have been overcome, and the Treasury received all the $16 million at no more than 7½ %.

Madison ordered a peace delegation to proceed to St. Petersburg to join Quincy Adams and wait there for Britain to send a delegation from its side. The U.S. delegation sat there for months, but there was no response: the British did not want to negotiate peace at all, much less accept Russian mediation in the process.

Foreign Minister Castlereagh wrote to Lord Cathcart, Britain's ambassador to Russia, July 5, 1813:

It [the mediation offer] has enabled the President to hold out to the people of America a vague expectation of peace... This evil, however cannot now be avoided, and it only remains to prevent this question from producing any embarrassment between Great Britain and Russia.

At that point, the British decided to make an offer: they would concede to direct negotiations with the U.S. representatives, but not in St. Petersburg, and not with any outside mediation. Adams wrote to Monroe, July 14 1813:

By Amédée Forestier, in the Smithsonian American Art Museum

John Quincy Adams (center right) shakes hands with British Baron Gambier at the signing of the Treaty of Ghent, ending the War of 1812.

My own information from private sources, and that of all the American and English here from their correspondents, concurs to show that the British government have been both surprised and mortified by the Emperor's offer of mediation... They do not appear at all to have foreseen that their most powerful and closest European allies would ever take any concern in a contest upon the question of impressments, and as a motive for declining the Russian mediation they have alleged that it was a dispute involving principles of internal administration, as if the United States were a mere appendage to the British dominions.

Even the offer of direct negotiations was a stalling tactic. The peace terms proposed by the British were outrageous and were designed to prolong the war, not end it. The British demanded an Indian buffer territory north of the Ohio River, the loss of U.S. fishing rights off the Newfoundland coast, and the expansion of Canada to allow access to the Mississippi River. One of the American negotiators, U.S. Senator Bayard, later stated "Their terms were those of a conqueror to a conquered people."

Nevertheless, although the St. Petersburg initiative did not result in an immediate peace treaty, the Russian intervention bolstered the financial credit of the United States government and sent a message to London that Russia would not tolerate an open-ended continuation of the war.

Rumiantsev continued to work with the American delegation. He relayed notes from Alexander, now traveling with his troops into Germany and Austria, notes that were still able to frighten the British. The British were worried that Alexander might demand that a discussion of the rights of neutral shipping be placed on the agenda for the upcoming Congress of Vienna, where post-Napoleon relations were to be worked out among the European states. The Congress of Vienna began in November 1814; on December 25, the British finally agreed to the Treaty of Ghent with the United States, with terms that seemed to restore the pre-war status quo. The Americans were happy to get what they could.

The Truth Will Out

The problem was that the United States was not really returned to the status quo of 1812. In the spring of 1812, the U.S. had a thriving shipping industry, which was increasing the power of the northern states, while the slave system of the southern states was actually in decline; in 1812, the U.S. was set to connect New York harbor with the Great Lakes states by finishing the Erie Canal, but funding for the Canal vanished during the war, and by 1815 it was a half-dug decaying ditch; and, in 1812, the U.S. had a world-historical relationship with the up-and-coming power of Europe—Russia. The American-Russian combination had represented a new kind of power bloc, not just one based on economic relations and geopolitical considerations, but a power bloc of the *mind*.

John Quincy Adams and Count Rumiantsev were the distillation of the best of their respective countries. They shared the excitement of a new world of possibilities for the growth and development of the human potential, as against the decay and denigration of the human spirit occurring in Old Europe.

After 1815, the British Empire had to make sure that such a strategic potential might never recur. The first step would be to rewrite the history of what had actually happened between America and Russia, to eradicate the truth about that partnership. And what better person to do the job than a direct descendant of John Quincy Adams?

Henry Adams' *History of the United States During the Administrations of Thomas Jefferson and James Madison* presented his grandfather as a weakling in the hands of cynical Russians and brilliant Englishmen. He writes,

[Adams] found a condition of affairs in Russia that seemed hopeless for the success of his mission. The alliance between Russia and France had reached its closest point. The Foreign Minister of Russia, Count Roumanzoff, officially known as Chancellor of the Empire, and its most powerful subject, favored the French alliance. From him Adams could expect little assistance in any case…and Adams soon found that at St. Petersburg he was regarded by France as an agent of England. He became conscious that French influence was unceasingly at work to counteract his efforts in behalf of American interests… Adams labored under the diplomatic inferiority of having to transact business only through the worse than neutral medium of Roumanzoff.

Henry Adams quotes, from his grandfather's diary, Lord Walpole's comments during the peace negotiations—as if John Quincy believed it:

[Lord Walpole] was as sure as he was of his own existence, and he believed he could prove it, that Roumanzoff had been cheating us all.

Henry Adams takes as proof of Rumiantsev's perfidy that Alexander had decided, after a couple of years traveling in the companionship of the likes of Nesselrode, Metternich, and Lord Cathcart (as they finished off Napoleon and began settlement negotiations in Vienna), to unofficially give Rumiantsev's functions over to Nesselrode. But at that point Alexander was once more in the grip of the British shipping empire, and was so financially strapped that he was taking subsidies from Britain to support his troops in Germany and France.

Rumiantsev's real problem was that he had tied himself totally to the Americans,— not that he had tied himself to Napoleon; and it was as a result of the weakening of American power during the War of 1812, that he had become an outcast, not because of the downfall of Napoleon.

In a letter to Monroe, Feb. 15, 1814, John Quincy Adams quotes Rumiantsev's own comments on his predicament, and then he takes his measure of the man:

'To be Chancellor of the Empire for the sake of signing passports and giving answers about law suits is not worthwhile… I can say that my heart is American, and were it not for my age and infirmities, I would now certainly go to that country.'

It was not the first time that the Count had suggested that the idea of going himself to America was floating in his mind. He had mentioned it before both to Mr. Gallatin and Mr. Bayard [treaty negotiators]…

The Count is a sincere and genuine Russian patriot. Of the statesmen with whom it has been my fortune to have political relations, I never knew one who carried into public life more of the principles and sentiments of private honor. His integrity is irreproachable; but his enemies are numerous… It is only in America that he could hope to find an asylum from the persecutions which will be the reward of his virtues and of his services to his country.

In February 2017, the promise of the Adams-Rumiantsev partnership has risen again. This time, it is the bankrupt and crumbling trans-Atlantic financial empire—the historic enemy of both Russia and America—that finds itself weak and besieged. Recent telephone discussions by President Trump with Vladimir Putin, Xi Jinping, and Shinzō Abe all point in the right direction. This time, the promise of 1812 stands ready to be realized.

European Politicians Still Blinded by Geopolitics

by Helga Zepp-LaRouche, chairwoman of the German political party
Civil Rights Movement Solidarity (BüSo)

Feb. 11—Among the great powers—the United States, China, Russia, Japan—totally new alliances based on mutual advantage are being built, which will potentially establish a higher level of reason and can effectively usher in a new era in history. In Europe, however, it has not yet been noticed by either the neocons and neoliberals or most of the left wing, and certainly not by the Greens, who are all so busy hyperventilating in various ways against U.S. President Donald Trump's victory, that they are numb to the major changes occurring on the political world stage.

Even such apparently staunch Atlanticists as Finance Minister Wolfgang Schäuble, faced with the new President of the United States, suddenly see hope in China's role — an almost delightful irony. The followers of the geopolitical doctrine in Europe are in a frenzy. They don't understand the world anymore. The Pippi Longstocking principle—"two times three is four, plus three make nine! I make the world the way I like it"—no longer works. The shock caused by the failure of the axioms of unipolar geopolitics is somewhat comparable to the superseding of the Copernican heliocentric conception of the world by Johannes Kepler's idea of a harmonic and complex universe.

After Trump's letter to Xi Jinping, followed by a further tele-

Hyperventilating: the German weekly's Feb. 4 issue.

phone conversation, which was described by the White House as "lengthy" and "extremely cordial," and during which Trump supported the One China policy of the United States, the perspective for constructive cooperation between the United States and China is developing. Indeed, with the Trump Administration, there is a chance that the United States will accept China's offer of a "new type of power relations," which was deliberately ignored by Obama. This new model of relations is based on the absolute recognition of sovereignty, respect for different social and political systems, noninterference in internal affairs of others, and mutually beneficial cooperation. So there should be no contradiction between Trump's "America First" and Xi Jinping's "Chinese dream."

Japan Offers Infrastructure

The visit of Japanese Prime Minister Shinzo Abe to the United States—who brought with him, among other items, an investment package that would create 700,000 jobs in the infrastructure sector—need not conflict in any way with the improved U.S.-China relations. Abe spoke of Japan's international expertise in building modern infrastructure, and offered to build a maglev line between Washington and New York, which would allow President Trump to go from the White House to Trump Tower in Manhattan in only one hour.

When a Japanese reporter's question implied that Trump would not defend Japan from "Chinese aggression," Trump's reply demonstrated that he would not be lured into the geopolitical trap: "I had a very, very good conversation, as most of you know, yesterday with the President of China. It was a very, very warm conversation. I think we are in the process of getting along very well. And I think that will also be very much of a benefit to Japan.... We have conversations with various representatives of China, I believe, that that will all work out very well for everybody—China, Japan, the United States, and everybody in the region."

Chinese companies financed the Ethiopia-Djibouti Railway and now provide training of local stewards, drivers and technicians, creating thousands of new jobs and nurturing railway expertise for the two African countries.

en.people.cn

In addition, Jack Ma, the president of the Internet ecommerce firm Alibaba, and President Trump have already discussed Chinese investments of a trillion dollars, and there is great interest in further investments in the upgrading of American infrastructure.

Another indication of the new strategic orientation is that Prime Minister Abe intends to travel to Russia twice this year, and has reached an agreement with Russian President Putin for close collaboration in the economic development of the disputed Kuril Islands. This cooperation, along with significant investments by Japan in Russia's Far East, should strengthen trust, and create the preconditions for the signing of a peace treaty between the two nations. Among these investments are the intensification of cooperation in the development of crude oil and natural gas, the construction of new airports and ports, the modernization of agriculture, and the construction of urban infrastructure, water systems and canals, and a medical center.

The Trump White House, moreover, made known through a "senior Administration official" that the United States has nothing against the growing cooperation between Japan and Russia, but fully understands that these two neighbors want to improve their bilateral relations.

Also, President Trump's repeated declaration that he wants to establish a good collaborative relationship with Russia, is finding a positive echo from the Russian side. In an interview with *Izvestia* published Feb. 10, Foreign Minister Sergey Lavrov expressed confidence that the forging of a constructive and mutually beneficial relationship between the two countries would be very advantageous for the Russian and American peoples, and thus have a positive effect on the whole world situation.

Meanwhile, the Russian ambassador to China, Andrei Denisov, let it be known that President Putin would participate in the major summit on the Belt and Road Initiative that China will host in Beijing in May. China is preparing this summit, which aims at consolidating the policy of the New Silk Road, with great intensity. Senior diplomat Yang Jiechi stressed to *China Daily* that twenty heads of state have already agreed to attend, among whom, according to Professor Wang Yiwei, author of a book on the New Silk Road, is President Trump; this is a visit which the Chinese eagerly anticipate.

To the degree that the large Asian countries and the United States overcome previous geopolitical conflicts, the chances will improve for other regions of the world, regions that have had proxy conflicts, to attain a positive outlook on the future. Thus Tim Collard, a columnist for the official Chinese government portal site,

China.org.cn, suggested that with the rise of China as a global economic power—supported by the Asian Infrastructure Investment Bank and the Belt and Road Initiative—its willingness to engage, for example, in the Middle East, also will increase. This could create an entirely new dynamic in the region.

The *New York Times* was even obliged, for a change, to publish an objective and positive article on Feb. 7 with the headline, "Joyous Africans Take to Rails, with China's Help," in which it not only described the newly opened rail line from Djibouti to Addis Ababa, which China financed and built, but also other projects in Africa. The new rail lines—the first step toward the long dreamed-of trans-African routes from the Indian Ocean to the Atlantic—have already changed the total dynamic, according to Aboubaker Omar Hadi, head of the port in Djibouti. China has vision.

Wikimedia Commons/Freud
Horst Seehofer, Minister-President of Bavaria and Chairman, Christian Social Union (CSU).

Germany's 'Awesome Opportunity'

Apparently Minister-President of Bavaria Horst Seehofer (CSU) has sensed which way the new wind is blowing. According to media reports, he is working on arranging a meeting with Trump and plans another visit to Putin. Chancellor Merkel on the contrary appears to be absorbed in her new role as defender "of the free West." She has just expressed, together with Polish Prime Minister Beata Szydlo, her opposition to any easing of the sanctions against Russia. The support of the Berlin government for the regime in Kiev is a scandal. Unfor-

CC/Ralf Roletschek
Martin Schulz (right) in 2014 when he was President of the European Parliament. At left is the then Italian President, Giorgio Napolitano.

tunately, the SPD's candidate for Chancellor, Martin Schulz, who as President of the European Parliament until very recently, is *the* representative of the EU establishment, has not shown any inclination to present a real alternative to Merkel in his geopolitical view of Russia and China.

In the upcoming campaign for the Bundestag, the BüSo will make every effort to point to the enormous potential Germany could actualize by cooperating with the United States, Russia, China, Japan, and many other countries, above all in the economic development of Southwest Asia and Africa. Germany now has the awesome opportunity to devise a foreign policy which is both in the best interests of Germany, and in harmony with what Xi Jinping calls the "community of common destiny for mankind." Germany's inventive spirit and engineering expertise, and the productivity of its *Mittelstand*—its small and medium-size industrial enterprises—are exactly what the development of the world requires, and its participation in the projects of the New Silk Road and in international scientific cooperation would massively improve the range of jobs available domestically. That means leaving behind low salaries and unproductive jobs to create highly skilled, productive employment, and thereby a higher living standard for all.

Since hyperventilating involves inhaling too much oxygen and exhaling too much carbon dioxide, all those who blame CO_2 emissions for climate change should calm down and stop looking at Trump, China, and Russia through geopolitical glasses.

President Trump Launches War on Drugs, But Must Target Drug Banks

by Michael Billington

Feb. 10—President Donald Trump has launched a deadly serious War on Drugs. On Feb. 8, in a speech before the Major Cities Police Chiefs Association (MCCA) in Washington, the President said that the drug scourge was destroying the potential of America's youth and America's future, and must be crushed, naming the newly installed Secretary of the Department of Homeland Security, Gen (ret.) John Kelly, as the man to lead the effort.

The following day, Trump issued an executive order naming the newly confirmed Attorney General, Jeff Sessions, to be head of a new Task Force "to focus on destroying transnational criminal organizations and drug cartels," with a 120-day mandate to report on "transnational criminal organizations and subsidiary organizations, including the extent of penetration of such organizations into the United States."

This is the first serious call for combatting the drug scourge—now devastating every community and millions of families in the United States—since Lyndon LaRouche first coined the term "War on Drugs" in 1980. The LaRouche organization then formed the "National Anti-Drug Coalition" and launched the magazine "War on Drugs."

The one problem with the Trump War on Drugs— and a potential Achilles Heel, if it is not corrected—is the failure to identify and target the actual core of the international drug cartel, the banks which facilitate this business. The publication by *EIR* in 1978 of the first edition and reprints of *Dope, Inc.* and the half-dozen subsequent editions and re-issues of that blockbuster exposé, documented in great detail how the illicit drug business—the biggest business in the world—is controlled entirely by the British and Wall Street banks, since the time of the British Opium Wars against China, and continuing through to today.

The identification of the too-big-to-fail banks in

Secretary of Homeland Security John Kelly testified that the U.S.A. has to shut down the drug trade.

London and New York as the headquarters of "Dope Inc.," will also provide yet another motivation for the immediate restoration of the Glass-Steagall Act, to stop the criminal money laundering and speculation which has brought the trans-Atlantic financial system to ruin.

President Trump is fully aware that the drug issue is central to the future of the nation, as was clear in his remarks to the Major Cities Police Chiefs Association Winter Conference in Washington on Feb. 8. He emphasized that "every child in America should be able to play outside without fear, walk home without danger, and attend a school without being worried about drugs or gangs or violence.... So many lives and so many people have been cut short. Their potential, their lives have been cut short. So much potential has been sidelined. And so many dreams have been shattered and broken, totally broken.

"It's time to stop the drugs from pouring into our

HSBC Bank

Dope Inc.: Run by British Banks

President Trump's War on Drugs is to be highly commended, and to be supported in full by all those anywhere in the world who treasure the human mind and human spirit, but it will fail if it does not go after the heart of the beast—the British banks, headed by HSBC, and its Wall Street subsidiaries. Under its earlier name—the Hong Kong and Shanghai Bank—HSBC ran the opium trade in Asia during the Opium Wars of the 19th Century, and more recently ran the money laundering for the Mexican drug cartels into the United States.

When HSBC was caught in this crime, the Obama Administration, busy promoting drug use and the legalization of drugs across the United States, ruled that no bankers should be criminally prosecuted for drug money laundering, just as none were to be prosecuted for the massive crimes in their derivative scams leading to the 2007-08 near collapse of the western banking system. Obama's ties to George Soros, the notorious funder and promoter of virtually every international effort to legalize drugs, are well-documented.

country," Trump continued. "And, by the way, we will do that. And I will say this: General—now Secretary—Kelly will be the man to do it."

He continued: "It's time to dismantle the gangs terrorizing our citizens, and it's time to ensure that every young American can be raised in an environment of decency, dignity, love, and support. You have asked for the resources, tools, and support you need to get the job done. We will do whatever we can to help you meet those demands."

The President noted that he had brought a number of law enforcement officials to the White House, and asked them "what impact do drugs have in terms of a percentage

swiss-image.ch/Michael Wuertenberg

Redesigning the International Monetary System: A Davos Debate 2011: George Soros.

President Trump is now positioned to correct this crime. He promised during his campaign to implement the Glass-Steagall Act—the Franklin Roosevelt law which separated commercial banks from investment banks, offering government support only to the former, which were forbidden to participate in speculative activities. President Trump must be held to account for that promise. If the Glass-

on crime? They said, 75 to 80 percent. That's pretty sad. We're going to stop the drugs from pouring in. We're going to stop those drugs from poisoning our youth, from poisoning our people. We're going to be ruthless in that fight. We have no choice.... And we're going to take that fight to the drug cartels and work to liberate our communities from their terrible grip of violence."

EIRNS/Dean Andromidas

Former UN official Antonio Mario Costa was simultaneously Executive Director of the United Nations Office on Drugs and Crime (UNODC) and Director-General of the United Nations Office in Vienna (UNOV) from 2002 to 2010.

Steagall Act is implemented, the drug money operations of the "too-big-to-fail" banks will be dried up virtually overnight, and the drug cartels can be mopped up relatively easily.

It is not only Lyndon LaRouche who has identified the role of the banks in the global drug trade. In 2009, after the 2008 near-collapse of the western banking system, Antonio Maria Costa, then the head of the UN Office on Drugs and Crime, pointed out that the international banks had become "drug dependent." He said: "In many instances, the money from drugs was the only liquid investment capital. In the second half of 2008, liquidity was the banking system's main problem, and hence liquid capital became an important factor. Inter-bank loans were funded by money that originated from the drug trade and other illegal activities... There were signs that some banks were rescued that way."

Viktor Ivanov, the Director of the Russian Federal Narcotics Service from 2008 until 2016, speaking in Washington in 2011, said: "Drug money and global drug trafficking are actually not just valuable elements of, but as donors of scarce liquidity, a vital and indispensable segment of the whole monetary system." In order to shut this down, he said, Russia and the United States must work in tandem to effect a "drastic transformation of the international financial system.... To a certain extent, we are observing a revival of the logic of the Glass-Steagall Act, adopted in the U.S. in 1933 at the height of the Great Depression, which separated the deposit and investment functions of banks."

However, he added, "restrictions to prevent the attraction of criminal money are required even more. In other words, liquidation of the financial bubble alone will not be enough.... The key way to liquidate global drug trafficking, is to reformat the existing economy and shift to an economy that excludes criminal money" and provides reproduction of net "liquid assets, i.e., to an economy of development, in which decisions are based on development projects and long-term targetted credits."

Trump's Executive Order vs. Dope, Inc.

Trump's executive order of Feb. 9 is powerful and clear: "Transnational criminal organizations and subsidiary organizations, including transnational drug cartels, have spread throughout the nation, threatening the safety of the United States and its citizens.... These groups are drivers of crime, corruption, violence, and misery.... In particular, the trafficking by cartels of controlled substances has triggered a resurgence in

en.kremlin.ru

Russia Federal Drug Control Service Director Viktor Ivanov, January 13, 2016.

deadly drug abuse and a corresponding rise in violent crime related to drugs.... A comprehensive and decisive approach is required to dismantle these organized crime syndicates and restore safety for the American people."

This executive order came at the same time as the confirmation by the U.S. Senate of Jeff Sessions as U.S. Attorney General. Sessions has been one of the fiercest opponents of the drug legalization policy implemented by Barack Obama.

It is also relevant that Gen. (ret.) John Kelly, the former head of U.S. Southern Command, who is now Secretary of Homeland Security, emphasized the importance of a "layered approach that extends far beyond our shores, throughout the hemisphere, in partnership with our neighbors to the South and North," when he testified before the Senate in January. "If the drugs are in the United States, we've lost," he said.

He estimated that 99% of the heroin that enters the United States is produced in Mexico. Poppies used to manufacture heroin are grown in Mexico and Guatemala, and then the drug is shipped to the United States. He emphasized the importance of a partnership with Mexico, saying the United States would like "to help them get after the poppy production... after the production labs... after the heroin, methamphetamine... before it gets to the border." It should be added that the destruction of the Mexican economy since NAFTA has left many of its youth with nowhere to go but the drug trade. There must be economic development.

On the U.S. side of the border, Kelly said the demand for drugs must be drastically reduced. "You're never going to get to zero," he said, "but we know how to do this. We've done it before with other drugs and other things that were bad for our society." Speaking of the Bush and Obama years, Kelly added: *We're not even trying."*

Join the Fight

President Trump's War on Drugs provides yet another stark reason for the hysterical campaign by London's Dope, Inc. to bring Trump down. A destabilization like the "color revolutions" run by drug-pusher George Soros against nations across Europe, Africa, the Mideast, and South America, is now being waged against the government of these United States, led by the City of London, its Wall Street subsidiaries, and their whorish presses.

The means to defeat this evil is to mobilize the American people, and people around the world, to induce President Trump to carry out his pledge to enact the Glass-Steagall Act, and restore the "American System" of Hamiltonian banking, capable of directing credit into national infrastructure, industrial and agricultural growth, and restoring the nation's dedication to advancing the frontiers of scientific knowledge, through fusion power development and space exploration—LaRouche's Four Laws.

The President has demonstrated that he is willing to work with the great nations of the world—Russia, China, Japan, and a restored Europe and America—to create an era of "Peace Through Development," as with Xi Jinping's "win-win" policy of the New Silk Road. By restoring America's role as a nation builder, and protecting the future of our children as productive and creative human beings, America can and must, once again, stand as a Temple of Hope and a Beacon of Liberty for the entire world.

Dark Figures   Part I of II

by Dennis Speed

And there were times when they said, Well the computer gave an answer, and it was so unexpected, they would ask me to check and see if that was the correct answer. And it either was, or it wasn't. And they accepted whatever I said.

—Katherine Johnson,
May 5, 2016, interviewed at Langley
Research Center in Hampton, Virginia

There was a time, when Americans still spoke literate English, that a computer referred to someone that computed, and not a machine. That was when human scientific insight, and imagination, was known to be the true domain of scientific discovery, for which mathematics was merely a useful tool.

In 1943, at the height of American involvement in World War Two, eleven African-American women from Hampton Institute in Virginia, were enrolled in a "war training class," called "Engineering for Women." They qualified for employment upon completion of the course, to work at the Langley Aeronautical Laboratory, part of what was called the National Advisory Committee on Aeronautics, or NACA—the precursor to NASA. They worked on assisting in the design of the safety aspects of the new aircraft being developed in the context of the war effort.

This was the beginning of the "human computer" unit of over 30 African-American women, led by scientist Dorothy Vaughn, that Katherine Johnson would join ten years later, in 1953. Johnson is credited with calculating the flight trajectory for Alan Shepard, the first American in space. The film *Hidden Figures* portrays her as the person most trusted by astronaut John Glenn, who refused to fly his

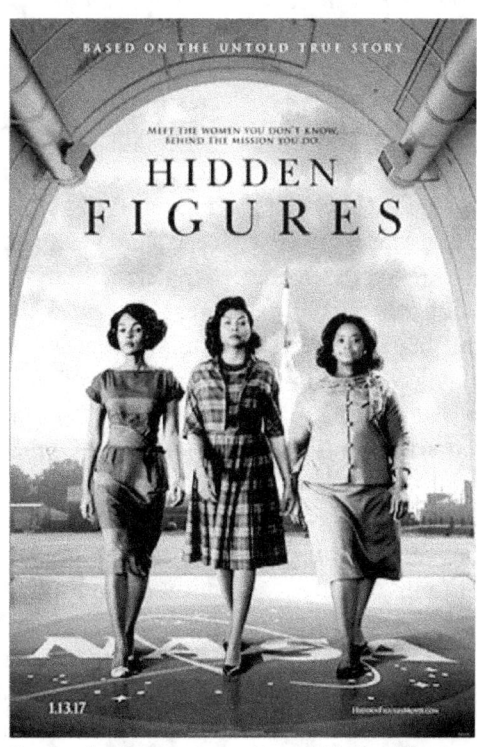

Poster for the movie version of Hidden Figures.

famous 1961 mission until the "machine computer's" contradictory figures were checked by human computer Johnson, referred to as "the smart one."

Mobilizing the Best Resources

Progress in America—or anywhere else, for that matter—is neither continuous, nor linear. The FDR era (1932-1945) was not the Hoover era—and also was not the Truman era. America was a better place after President Hoover's departure, and before Truman's arrival in the Presidency. Axiomatic change in America's institutions was necessary for its climb out of the Great Depression, and for the success of its two-front Japan/Germany war effort. That "all hands on deck" mobilization of the best resources of the American people would see the United States develop the most successful economy in world history, as its fundamental and irresistible capability for defeating the forces of fascism worldwide.

FDR's three-plus term Presidency was fundamentally transformative for the United States as a whole, and for African-Americans in the United States, in particular. The Reconstruction-era promises of a better America, which had been stifled by 1876 and wiped out by *Plessy v. Ferguson* in 1896, were reborn.

This is beyond the immediate scope of the *Hidden Figures* movie, as well as the excellent eponymous book written by author Margot Shetterly. Yet, it must be revealed, such that the actual socio-historical context of the film, which is not a documentary, but a docu-drama, be acknowledged.

Aside from the well-known 1940s migrations of African-Americans to Northern cities like Chicago, Cleveland, Philadelphia, Hartford, and New York, to work in defense-related industries, in

Hampton, Virginia and a few other locations, something unique existed in the United States. Functioning industrial schools had either already been established, or were being established in "Historically Black Colleges" such as Tuskegee Institute. Ironically, it was precisely because of segregation that skills in "forbidden fields" for "non-credentialed" African-Americans, such as chemical engineering, were passed on and acquired by those that had "gone beyond the scope of the classroom."

Persons of genius such as George Washington Carver taught at these institutions and were temporarily allowed, starting in the 1930s, to emerge and flourish. These pools of developed and skilled capability were tapped for the war effort. The later, successful actions of the 1950s referred to as "the civil rights movement" were in large measure a resultant effect of the demonstrated excellence (as well as organizing skills) of the "War Generation" of Americans of African descent, such as the mechanical engineers and pilots that comprised the "Tuskegee Airmen."

'Most Successful Civil Rights March'

This was not unknown or lost on FDR. For example, Eleanor Roosevelt championed them, going out of her way to ride in an airplane piloted by a Tuskegee Airman, at a time when it was asserted that African-Americans were not intelligent enough to fly planes, especially in combat over the European theater.

Those later, still-famous 1950s actions were preceded by the 1940s work of people such as activist Asa Phillip Randolph, including his threatened March on Washington, which he issued the call for in May of 1941:

> With faith and confidence of the Negro people in their own power for self-liberation, Negroes can break down that barrier of discrimination against employment in National Defense. Negroes can kill the deadly serpent of race hatred in the Army, Navy, Air, and Marine Corps, and smash through and blast the Government, business, and labor-union red tape to win the right to equal opportunity in vocational training and re-training in defense employment.
>
> Most important and vital of all, Negroes, by the mobilization and coordination of their mass power, can cause *President Roosevelt to issue an Executive Order abolishing discriminations in*

Paving The Way For Women Engineers

Above are shown members of the first women's class in engineering fundamentals at Hampton Institute, who will complete their 10-week course on May 8. Under the supervision of Dr. B. A. Turner, the course qualifies students for civil service appointments as junior engineers, at $2,000 annually. In the photo are, left to right, front row, Miss Madelon Glenn of Hartford, Conn.; Mrs. Lucille Hibbler, Newport News; Miss Minnie McGraw, Columbia, S. C.; Miss Mary Cherry, Windsor, N. C.; Mrs. Miriam Mann, Hampton; second row, Misses Jean Sampson, Hampton; Mabel Slickle, Hampton; Pearl Bassette, Phoebus; Mrs. Thelma Stiles, Hampton; Miss L. Lucille Leath, Burlington, N. C.; and Mrs. Ophlia Taylor, Hampton. Applications will soon be available for qualified women college graduates to enroll in the second series of courses in this work which will begin at Hampton on June 15, Dr. Turner said this week.

A newspaper story on the first eleven African-American women enrolled in 1943, in a war training class in engineering fundamentals.

all Government Departments, Army, Navy, Air Corps, and National Defense jobs.

FDR issued Executive Order 8802 on June 25, 1941, creating the Fair Employment Practices Committee. Randolph, NAACP head Walter White, and others had not given a date for their march, which never occurred. Thus, the 1941 March On Washington is often referred to as "the most successful civil rights march that never happened." African-American federal employment increased from 60,000 in 1941 to 200,000 in 1945. The war, which was declared five months after the FEPC was created, was the forcing medium, despite the continuation of segregation in the armed forces and other areas.

Hidden Figures uses various dramatic devices to demonstrate that the fact that they were accepted as employees at Langley Research Center did not mean that African-American employees did not have to fight daily for their dignity. This, however, did not begin in the 1950s, as the movie might seem to suggest, but from the very beginning in 1943. *Hidden Figures* omits the story of Miriam Mann, a member of the West Computers group (the euphemism used for the segregated African-American women computers at NACA) who would daily, in the early 1943, steal the *colored computers* sign in the cafeteria, risking being fired in the legally segregated state of Virginia. The sign would reappear each day, and she would steal the sign again, to the consternation of her fellow computers. Day after day, month after month, this continued. One day, it was not replaced, and therefore no longer needed to be stolen.

Hidden Figures has become an unexpected national sensation. It is a rare combination: an intelligent film that also makes money. Nominated for three Academy Awards, it has grossed about $127 million dollars in the United States and Canada. Its cast was honored at the 23rd Annual Screen Actors Guild Awards.

Katherine Goebel Johnson, prominently featured in the film as portrayed by actress Taraji Henson, received the Presidential Medal of Freedom in 2015, and had a NASA building named after her—the Katherine G. Johnson Computational Research Facility—in May 2016. The building will open this year, which is also the 100th anniversary of the establishment of the Langley Research Center of the NACA.

Scientists Were 'Normal People'

At the Screen Actors Guild Awards, in the acceptance speech for "best cast in a motion picture," Henson said:

> This film is about unity. We stand here as proud actors… but the shoulders of the women that we stand on, are three American heroes—Katherine Johnson, Dorothy Vaughn, Mary Jackson. Without them, we would not know how to reach the stars. These women did not complain about the problems, their circumstances, the issues. We know what was goin' on in that era. They didn't complain. They focused on solutions. Therefore, these brave women helped put men into space. We cannot forget the brave men that also worked with us. God rest his soul in peace, John Glenn!! This story is of unity. This story is about what happens when we put our differences aside, and we come together as a human race. We win, Love wins, every time. Thank you so much for appreciating the work we've done. Thank you so much for appreciating these women. They are hidden figures no more.

TV interviewer Femi Oke asked Margot Shetterly, author of the book *Hidden Figures: The American Dream and the Untold Story of the Black Women Mathematicians Who Helped Win the Space Race,* the question, "Did you feel special when you were growing up?" She replied:

> I didn't, and I think that was the best part about it. It was middle America. My parents got up, they went to work every day. My dad happened to work at NASA. Everybody worked at NASA. I knew some of the ladies that I write about in the book. And they happened to be very good at their jobs—mathematicians, scientists, engineers. They were also just normal people. So for me, I got an up-close look that science could be done by anyone—by normal people, by people that I knew. It was something that was literally living in my neighborhood.

Of course, Shetterly's world is far different than the world of the 1940s or 1950s about the which she writes. She was born in 1969, after the assassinations of JFK, Malcolm X, Martin Luther King, and Robert Kennedy. Her father was born in 1944, and was told by his father that his highest higher educational aspiration should be to become a physical education teacher. Instead, he studied electrical engineering at Norfolk State College. This was the era of John F. Kennedy and his idea of "sending a man to the moon and returning him to earth safely within the decade." It is difficult to explain to those born after 1980 what the slain President Kennedy and his Apollo Project actually meant to the country, and to people like her father.

This is in no way, however, to cast aspersions on the movie, which should be seen, and the book, which should be read. At particularly this moment in America, such a shared cultural experience can prove essential to the tasks before us. A new space program, returning to the Moon and exploring its far side, jointly conducted with China, Russia, India, South Africa and many other nations, would be the first step, and a great step to be taken by our nation at this time. The creation of a World Land-Bridge for global economic development, and the investigation of the world's atmosphere for purposes of deploying the "rivers in the sky" for use on earth, are only a few of the areas to be investigated, utilizing the yet to be discovered and cultivated capabilities of young women and men of all backgrounds.

Hidden Figures makes it clear that the scientific and technological optimism that has always been at the heart of the success of the American experiment is the only basis for durable change in our country, now as then.

Norbert Brainin on Motivführung

by Lyndon H. LaRouche, Jr.

The following was first published in the Sept. 22, 1995 issue of Executive Intelligence Review, *following—and related to—the Sept. 1, 1995 publication of La-Rouche's "That Which Underlies Motivic Thorough-Composition," reprinted last week.*

A potentially misleading turn of phrase was included in a picture caption, on page 51 of the Sept. 1 edition of **EIR.** The relevant passage reads: "…Norbert Brainin, the first violinist of the former Amadeus Quartet, and a collaborator with LaRouche in the development of the concept of motivic thorough-composition." In fact, Norbert Brainin presented the notion of *Motivführung* to me, through a mutual friend, just over four years ago. Summarily, this came about under the following circumstances.

During 1990, I had posed to my collaborators the proposition, that the benchmark for the organization of the second book of the **Manual on the Rudiments of Tuning and Registration**[1] ought to be the revolutionary change in the structure of musical composition represented by the comparison of the work of Josef Haydn to his predecessor Carl Philip Emmanuel Bach. Shortly after that, cellist Renée Sigerson had travelled to Germany, where she reported my proposal to Norbert Brainin. As Mrs. Sigerson reported this to me shortly afterward, Mr. Brainin had exclaimed, *"Motivführung,"* and followed that with an explanation of his meaning of that term.

My reaction to Mrs. Sigerson's report of this exchange, was one of great excitement.

During the late 1940s, I had first learned what every student of the Classical keyboard repertoire knows as the signal debt of Wolfgang Amadeus Mozart to Johann Sebastian Bach's **A Musical Offering**. For the keyboard repertoire, the key point of reference is Mozart's Köchel 475 Fantasy, prefaced to the Köchel 457 Sonata. From that point on, the K. 475 Fantasy is the most frequent point of variously direct and indirect reference met in the major keyboard and other compositions of Mozart, Beethoven, Schubert, and Brahms, among others.

Brainin's identification of the echoing of the Haydn Russian Quartets, notably Opus 33, No. 3, in the new method of composition presented by Mozart's six Haydn Quartets, transformed everything I knew about the implications of the Mozart K. 475 Fantasy. Putting those implications together with Brainin's *Motivführung,* revolutionized everything I knew about music axiomatically. Within weeks of receiving Renée Sigerson's report of the discussion in Germany, each nook and cranny of my previous knowledge of motivic thorough-composition was completely overhauled.

The result is to be recognized readily in a reading of my "Mozart's 1782-1786 Revolution in Music," published in the Winter 1992 edition of the **Fidelio** quarterly.

The reader would be greatly mistaken, if he or she imagined that this criticism of the referenced caption's potentially misleading ambiguity were merely a quibble. It is one of the commonplace disasters produced by modern textbook modes of education, that holders of terminal degrees of professional learning often lack competent insight into the most important considerations in the real history of ideas. As a case in point, consider summarily my own single fundamental discovery, known today as "The LaRouche-Riemann Method," effected over the course of the years 1948-52.

Axioms and Principles

Prior to 1952, I had made what has turned out to have been one of the most important scientific discoveries of this century, a fundamental principle of the science of physical economy. This discovery has been summarized in various locations over the years, most recently in "Why Most Nobel Prize Economists Are Quacks"[2] and "Non-Newtonian Mathematics for

---

1. See, **A Manual on the Rudiments of Tuning and Registration**, John Sigerson and Kathy Wolfe, eds. (Washington, D.C.: Schiller Institute, 1992). The project, of writing a two-volume manual, targetted by design for the use of music teachers and advanced students, was begun in 1985, but delayed by unexpected interruptions of the 1986-89 interval. The commitment to complete the then almost-finished Book 1 (on the singing voice), and to proceed with Book 2 (on the instruments), was summoned in 1990.

2. *EIR*, July 28, 1995.

Economists."[3] This discovery led, in turn, to a fresh view of the discoveries of Georg Cantor, and, that, in turn, to a fresh view of the most fundamental discovery of Bernhard Riemann, as set forth in his famous **Hypotheses** dissertation. In short, it was not a study of Riemann's dissertation which led me to my discovery in economics, but, rather, my discovery in economics made possible a revolutionized view of the implications of Riemann's discovery for economics. It was as if Riemann had written his **Hypotheses** dissertation as a contribution to the application of my discoveries in physical economy. Thus, my work is known by the epithet "LaRouche-Riemann Method," rather than "Riemann-LaRouche Method."

Similarly, just as my discovery in economics revolutionized Riemann's discovery, so, it was Norbert Brainin's discovery which revolutionized my knowledge of music. My earlier understanding of the implications of Mozart's reworking of Bach's **A Musical Offering**, as in his K.475 Fantasy, or Beethoven's Opus 111 Sonata, was the relatively commonplace knowledge of all qualified musicians. The addition of one ingredient, Brainin's identification of the implications of the germ-principle in motivic thorough-composition, transformed everything which I knew of music up to that time.

Norbert Brainin's revolutionizing my knowledge of music, in that way, like my own revolutionizing of the implications of Riemann's **Hypotheses** dissertation, involves the addition of a fundamental principle to the implied set of axioms underlying an existing body of knowledge. The addition of one principle revolutionizes everything.

Briefly, then, the following qualifying remarks are to be added here.

Every effort to represent an existing body of knowledge as logically consistent, restricts all acceptable propositions in that field to an array of theorems which are each and all consistent with one another, and also consistent with an underlying set of axioms, analogous to the axioms of a formal classroom geometry. Such a set of axioms is known among literate persons as an *hypothesis*; this is the usage of the term "hypothesis" by both Plato and Bernhard Riemann, for example, in contrast to the illiterate use of the same term in Isaac Newton's famous *"hypotheses non fingo."* Any change within the set of axioms associated with a specific hypothesis, produces a second hypothesis which is abso-

Norbert Brainin, first violinist of the former Amadeus Quartet, with pianist Günter Ludwig.

lutely inconsistent with the first.

In rigorous scientific usage, the distinction between an ordinary discovery and a fundamental discovery, is that every fundamental discovery represents a change in the existing set of axioms, and, therefore, the generation of a new hypothesis. In mathematics, such a change in hypothesis marks an absolute mathematical discontinuity (contrary to the mystical, reductionist sleight-of-hand, respecting discontinuities, of Leonhard Euler, Cauchy, the Bourbaki group, et al.). Thus, for me, Norbert Brainin's presentation of his view of *Motivführung* represented a sweeping discovery, a new axiom, and, therefore, a new hypothesis.

Of all such discoveries, whether one initiates them oneself, or learns them from another, one echoes Archimedes, crying out, "Eureka!" All is changed, as if in a single instant.

My distinctive advantage in receiving this knowledge from Brainin, lay in the fact, that unlike most who shared my earlier knowledge of the musical side of the matter, my prior discoveries in economic science supplied me relevant knowledge of the human creative-mental processes. Thus, my first published presentation on this subject appeared as the second of a series of articles on the principle of metaphor in science. So, I have situated the implications of Brainin's representation of that principle of composition since.

Thus, whatever the *Brotgelehrten* might think of such matters, we who treat ideas seriously, prefer to be precise about such matters. That is the difference in point of view between the person whose world-outlook, like my own, is shaped by a Classical-humanist (e.g., Platonic) outlook, and the less fortunate fellows whose opinion has been shaped by a textbook-oriented education.

---

3. *EIR*, Aug. 11, 1995.

Take It from
An Old Mountain-Climber

Feb. 14—What makes history happen? What is it that dictates that it comes out this way, rather than another way? Do you really believe your professors with their doctrines of the "immaculate conception" of history? That is, doctrines of history determined by trends, by "isms," by the *Zeitgeist* or some other chimera? By statistics? Even if that whole fairy-tale were all true—how could *they* possibly know that, when all they have ever done about it is to read the books written by other professors?

The profound changes in world history caused by Lyndon LaRouche's guidance of President Ronald Reagan and of Reagan's 1981-89 Administration, prove how history is actually shaped in the real universe in which we live, outside of the schoolroom. This becomes a far-reaching proof of principle, a "unique experiment," once you realize that it was only the London-directed sabotage of the LaRouche-Reagan "Strategic Defense Initiative" (SDI), which doomed us to the subsequent wretched decades of darkness under the Bushes and Obama. But for the 1980s British sabotage against the SDI, the Reagan Administration would actually have led the way into a new world of a peaceful alliance of almost all nations, dedicated first and foremost to "the common aims of mankind"—on Earth and in the universe at large. By now, poverty and war would have been things of the past, and mankind would be mastering the Solar system—however strange all that may sound to you today.

This is an immediate practical question now, during the first weeks of 2017, when once again we can see the prospects for leaving behind what Helga Zepp-LaRouche calls the "childhood of mankind," after our recent unnecessary decades in Hell. This whole issue is immediately relevant because of the great potential power for Good of the institution of the U.S. Presidency, as it was designed by Alexander Hamilton.

When Lyndon LaRouche was co-opted into a patriotic group of Franklin Roosevelt veterans, who were preparing the incoming Administration of Ronald Reagan, LaRouche was already an accomplished scientist, who had made original discoveries which would have lived on through future ages—even if he had put his typewriter away forever at that moment. But he didn't stop there. All of his enormous contributions to the Reagan Administration, were original, unique solutions to new problems which had never before existed in that form. There was no recipe; he was like Alexander the Great improvising on the battlefield.

His development of the manifold strategy to which the President gave the name of the "Strategic Defense Initiative" (SDI), gave us the means to put an end to the madness of "Mutually Assured Destruction," the balance of nuclear terror—a problem totally new to human history. At the same time, if the SDI had been adopted and not sabotaged, it would have ended the consignment of the "Third World" to permanent misery, while leading towards the superseding of adversarial hostility of the "First" and "Second" worlds. In brief, LaRouche's and Reagan's plan called for the creation of devices based on new physical principles, which would render thermonuclear weapons "impotent and obsolete." The U.S. would share this technology with the then-Soviet Union, and both sides would use these new powers to rapidly upshift their economies and to develop the so-called "underdeveloped" nations.

LaRouche cut the Gordian knot.

Not just the SDI, but also LaRouche's design of "Operation Juárez" during the early Reagan years, and his other contributions, were all, as we said, original creative solutions to new, unprecedented problems. As was all of Alexander Hamilton's advice to the George Washington Administration which he had done so much to shape. And both of these great scientists put not merely their entire careers and their reputations on the line, for the truth of what they knew to be true. They put their lives on the line. Hamilton was killed for his efforts on behalf of humanity. LaRouche was nearly killed—President Reagan derailed a plot against LaRouche's life at the last minute, after which LaRouche was framed up and railroaded to prison for five years.

The question for you is as old as Plato's *Theaetetus* dialog—one which LaRouche solved afresh in the long-ago 1950s. Do you really know what you think you know? How can you get to what is actually true? What is the real truth—the truth you will stake your life on?

The air gets pretty thin up there at the top of the mountain. Lyndon LaRouche, a mountain-climber from his youth, used to recall the experience of arriving at the top of the mountain, past the tree-line, where suddenly everything becomes visible for miles around, "and you're responsible for everything you see," as he said.